Three Old Motorcycles
Reflections from a Thousand Mile Journey

Chuck Granata
Illustrations by Susan Szecsi
Photographs by Scott Durrwachter

Copyrights

Three Old Motorcycles
Reflections from aThousand Mile Journey
By Chuck Granata

First Edition 2018
Hardcover ISBN: 978-0-9998742-0-2
Paperback ISBN: 978-0-9998742-1-9

Copyright © 2018 Chuck Granata
chuckrt66@gmail.com

Edited by Ana Manwaring
www.anamanwaring.com

Illustrations and book design by Susan Szecsi
www.brainmonsters.com
Photographs by Scott Durrwachter
Cover photo: Steve in the White mountains

© All rights reserved. No part of this publication may be reproduced, stored in a retrieval system, or transmitted in any form or by any means electronic, mechanical, photocopying, recording, or otherwise, without the prior permission of the copyright owner.

Printed in the USA

For

Steve Kielar and Scott Durrwachter

my forever friends and brothers

Contents

06	Morning Greetings
12	South Lake Tahoe
22	Virginia City
32	The Bristlecone Pines
48	Yosemite
60	Home
74	Epilogue

Illustrations and Photographs

06	Napa Valley – illustration
12	Lake Tahoe – illustration
21	Dreaming – illustration by Chuck Granata
22	Virginia City, Nevada – illustration
32	Bristlecone Pines – illustration
40	Old Stone Dwelling – photograph
41	Overlook at Mono Lake – from left to right, Steve, Scotty, Chuck – Lee Vining, California – photograph
43	Cactus Flower in the White Mountains – photograph
44-45	Looking west to the Sierra-Nevada Mts. from White Mts. – photograph
46	Steve nabbing the moon – photograph
49	Tuolumne Meadows, Yosemite National Park – illustration
59	Tuolumne Meadows – photograph
60	Napa Valley – illustration
69	Pete – He didn't get to go – photograph by Daphne Birkmyer
70	Motorcycles in the Sonoma Valley – photograph
71	Breakfast at The Fremont Diner – Chuck, Scotty and Steve – photograph
72	Rainbow over The Great Basin, from Virginia City – photograph
73	Steve and Chuck in Tuolumne Meadows – photograph
74	Sailing Ship – illustration
77	Fireworks over Stinson Beach, California – illustration

"I enjoy the morning starts the most—the first ride of the day—we're fresh (usually), happy and eager to be on the road again and off on another adventure."

Chuck Granata, *Three Old Motorcycles*

Morning Greetings

Early on a summer's morning, wearing deerskin gloves and a leather jacket, I ride the back roads out of Napa beneath the cool and shadowy live oak canopies that overhang these narrow ways. Grazing cows and horses barely blink as my motorcycle softly rumbles past—and up, over and down the hill through a long tunnel of trees and into a vineyard valley. An old red field tractor and pull-tank whine and clatter between rows of vines—leafy green shoots flutter in a swirling yellow cloud of pure, fine sulfur dust. A sweet, acidic, almost therapeutic smell lingers.

Arriving at the diner early, I buy a cup of strong hot coffee—sit and wait at the outdoor bar while cars whoosh along the country highway. The paper cup warms my hands until rays of sunshine spill over the eastern hills and fill the valley. I turn and face the sun as it crowns full above the hilltop—open my jacket wide and welcome in its warmth.

Cool coffee dregs swirl at the bottom of the cup. Low muffled rumors echo in the distance—the rumblings grow. I look west down the highway as Steve and Scotty ride into view. And the day begins.

* * *

Three weeks ago, in early June 2015, Steve finds me at work, "Chuck-man . . . we got it, the week of the twenty-ninth. You still good?"

"Definitely."

"Good man." He plants a hand solidly on my shoulder. "Let's do this. Today, four o'clock in the dining hall—you, me and Scotty."

"I'll be there."

At 4PM, I walk into the dining hall. Scotty and Steve are standing at the coffee station, chatting—steam still rising from the cups in their hands. Steve shouts, "Chuck-man."

"Steve, Scotty."

Scotty looks up from his phone, "What's hap'nen?"

"Not much Scotty." I grab an empty cup from under the counter and ask, "So where do you guys wanna go?"

Scotty says, "Virginia City'd be sweet. Stay a night in Tahoe at Mallory's?"

Steve raises both eyebrows, eyes wide open and points to Scotty and me, "And ride back through Yosemite."

"Yeah!" I chime, "Let's do it—there's a place in Sonoma we can meet for breakfast . . . and a back-way to Route 80."

Scotty smiles, "Cool."

Steve drops a hand on each of our shoulders, "Way t'go boys, Monday the 29th."

That's it. We'll sort out the rest later. We've been talking-up this road trip for months, itching to ride a real ride, far away from the San Francisco Bay Area traffic—new places, new experiences, and now we'll have a week to do just that.

* * *

Steve is all-accepting and gregarious. Scotty is thoughtful and creative. They're college rugby teammates, in their thirties, reliable and good-heartedly heedless. I'm in my sixties, cautious and reserved—a loner at heart.

However, Steve is a catalyst. His Thursday music-night parties were the scene for quite some time. I found them irresistible. Friends and friends of friends crowded in—everyone participating in their own way. There were hand drums, rattles, sticks and clapping, always guitars, sometimes flutes, rapping, singing, dancing and listening. The music was spontaneous, heartfelt and uplifting—on occasion, magical. A contingent spun off and formed a band—a band that Steve nudged into existence, a band that I play in, at clubs and at parties, which is somewhat out of character for me.

Steve and Scotty revel in the joy of motorcycling. One day I agreed with them, "Yeah . . . I *should* start riding again."

If I ran into Scotty at work, he'd show me pictures on his iPhone of motorcycles from *Craigslist*. He'd say, "Check this out."

It wasn't long before Steve drove with me to the East Bay to pick up the bike that caught my eye. Now, after a twenty-plus year hiatus to raise children—I do ride again.

This spring, Scotty enrolled in a motorcycle maintenance class at the City College extension in San Francisco. I joined him in the undertaking. The cost of repair shop maintenance is outrageously high, and who could care as much about my bike as I do? It was time to take responsibility.

Steve, Scotty and I had housing with our jobs—I lived in the Marin Headlands four days a week. On the mornings of our class, Scotty and I would ride along the cold, foggy cliffs above the ocean, cross the Golden Gate Bridge and weave our way through downtown San Francisco in rush-hour traffic. Andy, our instructor is an old codger like me and he's been riding and working on motorcycles most of his life. He instilled us with confidence and made the class fun. The shop was well-equipped with tools, lifts and old motorcycles to take apart and bolt together, or we could bring our own bikes in to work on. Class ended at noon. Scotty and I would ride back, usually under blue skies and sunshine, around the ballpark, along the Embarcadero, through the marina and back again across the bridge and into work.

* * *

Yet, for all my new-found inspiration, this morning, the day of our ride, as I stood barefoot in my garage in a clutter of carefully selected clothes, camping gear, mechanic's tools and spare motorcycle parts—I felt apprehensive, unsure whether I could keep up with the boys if they began weaving through traffic and splitting lanes like they like to do, or fly down an open highway at ninety miles per hour, which they said they wanted to do—and I was uncertain if our nearly forty-year-old motorcycles could make this trip without a break-down. Yet, more than that, I felt fundamentally responsible for Steve and Scotty—ironically, I knew they felt the same toward me. It's not really a father-son thing, because all men are children, even old men—especially old men. It's about friendship, and the responsibility that accompanies it—the yin and yang of respect.

While my old BMW touring bike stood stoically by waiting to be readied, Pete wandered in. Pete is a good-natured black and white spaniel with a tri-colored face. He sniffed through the clutter, showing special interest in the sleeping bag and cooking gear—filled with smells of people, food and places. Pete makes me smile. He finished his inspection and I quickly stowed or tied down every item—I was unsure of our final destination or how we would fare, but this wasn't my first motorcycle road trip.

South Lake Tahoe

Steve and Scotty ride into view. I slide off the bar stool, signal and wave them toward the overflow parking down the lane and walk over to greet them. They back their motorcycles in beside mine, which I had nosed in an hour earlier—hop off their bikes with a greeting and hug, and laugh about how I never face my bike in the right direction. Scotty pulls a camera from his backpack and takes a photo anyway, of the motorcycles all lined up and loaded with gear—sitting in the wine country and ready to roll. And, so it is—we meet Monday for breakfast at *The Fremont Diner,* Route 121 between Schellville and Napa.

It's a perfect morning to begin an adventure—birds singing, warm and sunny—what could go wrong on a day like this? We join the company outdoors at the picnic tables and sit with the hills and vineyards of the Sonoma Valley, and enjoy a leisurely breakfast of biscuits and gravy and good coffee.

Scotty polishes his plate with his last bite of biscuit and says, "We should start every morning with the same breakfast."

And we do, more or less, most of the trip.

We ride north on 121, with full bellies, in the fresh air and sunshine—up and down through rolling vineyards, cresting hilltops in a sea of green:

north, south, east and west. We're in the heart of the cool Carneros wine appellation—Chardonnay and Pinot Noir country. In Napa, we zigzag on the outskirts of town and into a narrow winding canyon along old Monticello Road. A sweet woodsy scent fills the warm canyon air from the oaks that cover the hills—the day warms by the mile as we wind our way in. We descend sharply and follow the creek's course through a steep ravine. The air grows hot and thick. The oak and bay trees, resinous brush, flowering plants and ground cover, the wild grape and blackberry vines in chorus exude a rich and spicy wine-like fragrance—I breathe in deeply. We stop in some shade on the side of the road, take off our leather jackets, and pee. Scotty and Steve will ride on in T-shirts and sunscreen, but the day is so clear and bright, I dig out a lightweight long sleeve shirt to ride in—and we're off again, cool and comfortable, shirtsleeves flapping in the wind as we round Lake Berryessa and drop into the valley and farmland and the small town of Winters, where Maggie is from.

"Maggie," and I quote an old friend, "has the voice of an angel." She once worked with us in the Marin Headlands. When cleaning the dining hall, she moved with long quick strides and bouncing hair—carrying trays of food, coffee pots and pitchers of cream while singing to the tunes that the guys in the kitchen were playing. Carlos the chef kept a cool collection of 50's and 60's music—doo-wop, rock, Motown soul. Although Maggie was younger than the music, by far, she knew quite a few of those tunes.

It's straight up noon in old-town Winters. We come to a stop and

I feel the heat. Still sitting on the motorcycles, we shuffle our feet and roll the heavy bikes back against the curb, gently lean them onto their side stands and set out to find cold drinks. At a corner deli with tables and umbrellas on a deck above the street, we sip cold beer and I suggest, "Let's stop for a beer every day by noon." Well . . . we'll see.

From Winters, it's not far to Davis. Jen, our friend and sometimes riding buddy, and Christi live here and attend the UC, but they're gone for the summer or we'd stop for a beer. We roll through Davis and pick up I-80 East to Sacramento—skirt the busy city to the start of US 50 and cruise toward the Sierra Nevada Mountains and the old gold-rush town of Placerville.

It's hotter in Placerville. We ride around town, looking for a bar that Steve recalls but can't find now. He swerves out of the street into a parking lot, hops off his bike and steps into a bank, hoping to get directions. Scotty and I sit outside in the shade—lean back against the cool north wall and savor this summer foothills' afternoon.

Steve comes out, without directions—we jump back on our bikes and continue the search, spot a public parking garage and duck in out of the sun to re-group.

We meet a local meter man, who's hanging out and checking meters—but he hasn't heard of Steve's mystery bar either. With the motorcycles squeezed into a parking spot, we buy an hour's worth of time, walk around town and find a cool place, *Bricks Eats and Drinks,* with craft beers on tap, big juicy hamburgers with the works and, possibly, the best golden wedges of deep fried potatoes I've ever tasted.

Luckily the bartender saved me when I misread the menu and unknowingly tried to order a veggie burger. She smiled the sweetest smile and asked me kindly, "Is that what you really want?"

After lunch, Steve buys a pair of wire strippers in a second-hand store, and a generic switch for his motorcycle in an old-time hardware store—the original starter switch is still mounted on his motorcycle, but has bare copper wires dangling down. Steve starts his bike by turning the key and touching the wires together. Though, I think the more serious problem might be, his headlight doesn't work.

We continue east on US 50—it's still warm going, but cooling as we make our way into the shade of the mountains. The road meanders along the South Fork of the American River for many miles through a steep gorge, all grey and green with granite and trees. The cycles chug smoothly as they make the climb—the river bubbles and rolls down the hill behind us. Our road, which lies between the river and the uphill slope, has neither exits nor need for thought. We slowly drift apart—the surrounding serenity lulls me along, and bits and pieces of this morning's anxiety slough away and silently fall.

By late afternoon we reach Meyers, just south of Lake Tahoe, Scotty signals a turn. We follow him uphill, past houses and woods to the outside edge of a sheer mountain curve with panoramic views of a vast pine forest wilderness—hills beyond hills roll away and fade into a far and hazy horizon. The road pulls us back into neighborhoods and subdivisions and to Mallory's grandma's house. Mallory is Scotty's newfound love. Grandma lives in San Francisco and this is her vacation home, which she generously shares with friends and family. We pull into the driveway and kill the engines—a quiet end to a long day's ride and a satisfying feeling of accomplishment.

Scotty breaks the silence. "We can put the bikes away later—let's go in and get a beer." With little discussion and no debate, we grab backpacks, clothing and miscellaneous gear, and walk around to the front of the house. The house is vacant and the door is locked, but Scotty has a key. We leave our dusty shoes and bags in the hallway entrance, slip into our sandals and head upstairs through the kitchen and a sliding glass door to a moss-covered deck high in the trees. On his last visit here, Scotty filled the fridge with beer, which we now enjoy while relaxing in the shade of tall Ponderosa pines and their pleasant, beeswax fragrance in the cool mountain air.

Revitalized, we grab more beer—head downstairs through the basement, out through the garage and roll the motorcycles in for the night. In the basement game room, we play ping-pong and pool, and a fast-action game called poon. We play poon on the pool table, using our hands instead of cue sticks. Billiard balls streak wildly across the table and smash together with a Crack! as we run frantically end to end shouting, Shit! On most of my turns, the eight ball drops in a pocket or rolls to a stop and I'm obliged to call out my standing. I shout, "P" on one turn and "P-O" the next, then "Poo" and "Poon" and I'm out. I jump back fast and out of the way as Steve and Scotty battle on, the game isn't stopping for me. A ball leaps from the table, flies across the room and puts a small round dent in the sheetrock. I back up as far as I can—glad I'm just watching. It's an epoch game and it finally comes to an end with Scotty's wins.

There's remorse for the dent, but I tell the boys it's an easy repair and we plan a return in the fall. We clean ourselves up, and lacking both a car and a designated driver, Scotty locks the front door and we begin the long walk into town.

We walk down Pioneer Trail, a road on the western slope of a pine-covered hill. In places we can see Lake Tahoe. The evening is warm and serene—we pass silently in single file through the pines. The westering sunlight flashes and flickers in the trees—everything glows golden-green.

By dusk, we reach Lake Tahoe Boulevard as the daytime colors fade to grey. We stroll east along the quiet boulevard for several blocks to Stateline Avenue. I step off the curb, cross the street and over the state line—out of California and into Stateline, Nevada—into the bright and bustling casino resort town—a kaleidoscope of neon lights and flashing colors, boisterous voices and perfumed whiffs of fast-moving fun-seekers, and I freeze on the crowded Nevada corner, seized in the festive spell. A firm hand grips and shakes my shoulder, Steve's voice booms, *"Chuck-Man."* I turn and follow. The boys are on a mission. They're moving fast now, drifting in and out of casinos and I don't dare let them out of my sight. Boundaries are vague—in the street and in the casinos—everywhere is the same brightness, the same crowdedness and tonight, the same temperature, too.

We reach our destination at the back of a casino, there's an old mechanical horse race game with six small, painted metal ponies trotting around a big oval track. A dozen people can sit around on tall stools and place bets by dropping quarters into slots in the countertop—and that's where most of the quarters stay. As we play and lose, a plan bubbles up in my mind. I tell the boys, "We can beat this game." They grin, but we try it, and it works. We root our ponies on and our coffers grow. New players come and the seats are filled—the room resounds with cheers and shouts and the clink of quarters.

With the flood of new betting, our luck runs out, the plan goes south and the lightweights leave. But Steve, Scotty and I persevere and are well rewarded with tall pitchers of strong IPA—certainly a fair trade. The more we bet, the more they bring.

We bet all our quarters, drink the last pitcher of beer and head for home—but the night is still young.

Back on the dark side, our luck returns. We find an all-night market and enough money for food—we haven't eaten since lunch. Steve and Scotty rummage through the frozen food bin and surface with a small box of cheese enchiladas and another small box with six White Castle mini-burgers, each with a tiny piece of onion garnish. With our prize catch in tow, we begin the long climb back up Pioneer Trail

A long climb it is, as my legs traverse the steep unlit roadway in a happy random fashion and try to keep pace with Scotty and Steve, who track the straighter path. With Scotty's good guidance, we find our way home and straightaway he puts dinner in the oven. As the food warms, a chewy, feastful aroma wafts through Grandma's kitchen, and we sit and wait with watery mouths until Scotty deems that all is ready and sets our supper on the table. The food is barely cool enough to touch, but we wolf it all down and sit around, still hungry and I note with regret, "We should've bought more boxes of hamburgers."

Scotty smiles and nods, "Definitely, we should've bought more boxes of hamburgers."

"Definitely!" Steve ends the debate, jumps up and grabs a six-pack from the fridge. We head downstairs and play ping-pong and poon, and I drink even more beer, drinking as though I can drink with impunity, although something tells me I'll pay for this.

I wake in the night; the room is way too stuffy—I need fresh air, but can't get the windows open. I bumble down to the basement game room—cool night air on a whisper of moonlight spills in through the open windows along the top of the basement wall. Steve is in his sleeping bag asleep on the couch—Man . . . he's got the perfect spot.

In a small adjoining room, faintly lit in pallid light, a large leather lounge chair sits unclaimed. I sink into its depths for what's left of the night.

Dreaming

Virginia City

Daylight fills the room I'm in. I slide out of the chair and slip past Steve, who's still buried in his bag on the couch. The upstairs floor is also quiet—Scotty must be sleeping, too. I take a cool shower and go outside for a walk with the hope of diluting some of last night's fun. But the summer solstice was recently here, and this thin mountain air can't constrain the heat or glare of the midsummer sun and I turn back, defeated, and retreat to the cool quiet of Grandma's house.

Out of the sunlight and into the house, I climb the half-flight into the living room. Scotty is there, reading a book. He's draped comfortably across the arms of a big upholstered chair and looks up as I walk in. I shake my head in weariness—he smiles and returns to his book. Across the room, an empty couch with cushions calls me. I shuffle over and slip off my sandals—lie down and close my eyes . . . ponder last night and this morning's outcome. Had I left that stuffy room sooner, I could have gotten a better night's sleep and would certainly feel better now—hmmm.

From the hallway comes a thumping sound—I open my eyes and see the basement door swings wide. Out pops Steve with an armload of beer cans and a loud greeting. "Hey, how you boys doin'?"

Scotty echoes, "Hey," closes his book and gets up.

I lift a hand and wave it in silence. Steve smiles and shouts some more, "Chuck-Man, you still alive?"

I try to smile, but only manage another wave. Steve doesn't look concerned—he never seems rattled.

The assuring aroma of brewing coffee and the clangor and clank of beer cans being dumped in the nearby kitchen recycle bin taunt me. I wish I wanted a cup right now or had the sea legs to scurry around and help the boys clean. Almost any other morning . . . my eyes close with fatigue and guilt. I've got to get myself together for the Virginia City ride. I can't let the boys down, and I'm off to a bad start.

They finish the cleanup and I reluctantly get up. With the house restored to the shape in which we found it, except for a small dent in the drywall, no one would know we were here. We haul our belongings down to the garage and roll the motorcycles out to the driveway. Scotty is concerned that his bike is running hot. We flush the radiator and add fresh coolant, and give all the bikes a quick once-over. While tying down gear, Scotty suggests we take the longer way clockwise around the lake, until we join back up with US 50 and then ride on to Virginia City. We have plenty of time, the ride is scenic and we don't have far to travel today. We'll do it.

Our first stop is *Red Hut Café* in South Lake Tahoe for breakfast. Scotty and Steve order big plates of biscuits and gravy, and eat all their food with gusto. I order a short stack with two pancakes and almost get through most of one. Steve looks at my plate and the untouched cake, "Chuck-man, you gonna eat that?"

I shake my head, "Take it."

He reaches across the table and stabs it with his fork, drops it on his plate and cuts off half for Scotty.

On our way out of town, we stop in a secondhand store and Steve finds a long sleeve shirt to ride in. His neck and arms are crimson. Our expensive SPF-50 sunscreen doesn't work very well in the mountains while we ride so close to the sun, but his three-dollar, all-cotton, dress shirt should work fine. Scotty has fared the same as Steve, and pulls a faded old flannel from his pack.

We ride north out of town on Highway 89, enter the pines and slowly climb above Emerald Bay's green-blue water. Beyond the shallow bay, the deep-blue water of Lake Tahoe stretches away to the distant mountains.

In Tahoe City, at a three-way intersection, Route 89 turns left to Truckee. We turn right onto Route 28—ride northeast along the water and continue to work our way around the lake. Our progress slows as the morning unfolds—on the North Shore, the traffic crawls to a stop. We weave around cars and road work, spot a convenience market in Kings Beach and pull into the parking lot. I'm ready for a break. We buy snacks and Gatorade and sit outside on a log in the filtered shade of a tall and willowy pine. No one mentions 'drinking beer by noon' anymore.

A mile down the road, we cross into Nevada at the small town of Crystal Bay and continue on through Incline Village, a summer and winter retreat. The road curves south and follows the steep and rocky shoreline. This is the fourth straight year of drought in the west, and it shows in the exposed rocks between the roadway and the distant water's edge. The east shore traffic is light and the ride is cool and easy. We cruise quickly to the US-50 junction and once again roll east along the old transcontinental highway, which winds its way from West Sacramento, California to Ocean City, Maryland.

    The cool water and air of Lake Tahoe fall behind as we climb onto the dry western slopes of the Sierra Nevada Mountains. The afternoon is hot and the uphill grades are long and steep—both Scotty and Steve's '77 Honda Goldwings overheat. We stop, let them cool, ride on and stop, and work our way to the top of the final pass. The downhill run is easy and the even warm desert air feels refreshing as we breeze swiftly through it. We roll to the bottom of the mountain, into the Great Basin and the town of Carson City, Nevada—the state's capital.

    Now, to Steve and Scotty's credit, they resurrected their motorcycles from a truckload of miscellaneous Goldwing bikes and parts they bought on Craigslist and I bet Steve five tanks of gas he couldn't rebuild his motorcycle in a month. We stop for gas, which is on me and continue east along US 50 to the Virginia City turnoff.

    Nevada State Route 341 winds its way north into the mountains, through a historic silver mining area with perfectly conical hills of ancient mine tailings in subtle pastel colors, tall dilapidated structures that once processed ore, and a cornucopia of abandoned wooden buildings and shacks, derelict vehicles and old rusting mining equipment. The road continues through the frontier towns and small present-day communities of Silver City and Gold Hill.

On the outskirts of Virginia City, we pull over a final time for Scotty's bike to cool. Steve's bike is a little less temperamental than Scotty's, and my old '76 BMW boxer-airhead runs okay—I mess with it more than I should—Scotty would rather be riding than working on his bike and Steve falls somewhere in the middle, but any differences are moot. We ride together and stop together, as we travel place to place.

We hop a low barbed-wire fence, walk out to the top of a steep slope with a view of the valley, and sit on the hard-baked desert ground with savory-scented plants and dry summer grasses. Riding with others has always been the exception with me. I like the freedom of riding alone and deciding the where and when—but, now I'm beginning to enjoy these moments of sharing and compromise, discovery and surprise outside of my normal spheres, the adventure of being a Musketeer, "One for all and all for one." After all, Scotty and Steve did help me through last night and this morning. I lean back against a spindly tree, plick pebbles at a fence post and daydream of a brief adventure I shared on a quiet afternoon in the summer of 1969.

I was lackadaisically making my way home from a ride through the countryside of western New Jersey on my first motorcycle, a little Suzuki X6 Hustler. I caught a red light outside of Morristown. As the cross traffic moved through, I heard, felt and watched in my mirror, a huge, grumbling, ground-shaking pack of motorcycles with leather-clad riders moving in fast.

The leader pulls up even with me, an arm's length to my right, on a magnificent Harley Davidson chopper. I nod a greeting, which I'm not sure he responds to, as both he and his bike shake to the powerful and steady throb of the engine. The big V-twin Harleys, have the idle of a heartbeat, *ba-boom ba-boom ba-boom ba-boom.* His motorcycle is pure, pristine and perfect—all black and chrome with long, extended front forks, high swept-back handlebars and a 1200cc engine that is undoubtedly reworked to the bone. My body vibrates to its bouncing rhythm and the twenty or so similar bikes behind us. Although my motorcycle is small, it's fast, and I'm proud of it. It's also black and chrome, except for the two shiny brass peace symbols I made and attached to either side of the gas tank. This is the sixties.

Young and fearless, with an empty road ahead, I look at the biker and rev my engine—it screams like a cat, but he doesn't seem to notice. The cross-light turns orange—red—our light flashes green. I pop the clutch and shoot forward with my front wheel in the air. As it floats back to the ground, I spin the throttle wide open and I'm out in front for a blink of an eye, when there's a gut-wrenching explosion of sound—the floodgates burst. In a deafening roar, the huge Harley blasts past me, accelerating faster than anything I've ever witnessed, and this is the heyday of street racing and muscle cars: Corvettes, GTOs, Mustangs and the Chrysler Hemi. Within seconds, the once larger-than-life bike and rider virtually vanish before my eyes. I back off the gas, dumbstruck.

The forgotten gang, which had held back, crushes me in a tsunami of sound, vibration, heat and the smell of hot metal and exhaust. They thunder around me with thousands of un-muffled combustion-chamber detonations. Streaks of metallic colors and glinting chrome fly past in pursuit of their leader—all on Harleys, all in black leather jackets or vests, embroidered with symbols and names I no longer recall, except for their home, which happened to be in the direction we were heading—Newark, New Jersey.

    Scotty feels that his bike has cooled enough—we walk back to the road fire them up and roll into town from the west. The first place we come to is the *Sugarloaf Motel,* and we check into a room for the night. I shower away the day's grime and the last of last night's as well—don a clean shirt, a pair of shorts and my sandals, and I'm a new man. The owners are about to drive to Carson City for the evening. Aside from our motorcycles, there's only one car in the motel parking lot—looks like we'll have the place to ourselves.

    Virginia City is terraced on the south-east slope of a mountain, more than six thousand feet above the floor of Great Basin. From the picnic table outside our room, we can see far to the south. Steve and I cross the street for even better views of the surrounding hills, the basin and mountains beyond. Scotty grabs his camera—he's the photographer in our party, and a good one as well.

    Storm clouds roll in from the east and crowd into the basin, where only two hours ago we rode through in fair weather. Above the distant grey and misty valley, two magnificent rainbows appear. They rise above the hills from out of the storm and soar nearly straight upward toward the zenith.

Steve and I return to the picnic table where Scotty is already waiting. He greets us with a smile and a deck of cards, a score pad and a pencil, and a bottle of extra special Irish Whiskey he's been saving for this journey. We pour the whiskey, deal the cards and pack a bowl of weed—settle into ringside seats—play gin rummy and watch the basin boil.

Jagged blue-white streaks flash up and out of the storm—sizzle, crackle—KA-BOOM—rumble, tumble and fade away—though we sit warm and dry, high on a mountain, under a clear cerulean sky. Evening comes, the rainbows fade and we walk down C Street into town.

Virginia City is an 'Old West' silver mining town. The main street is long and narrow. The buildings are made of wood, brick and stone, with wide covered porches held up by thick wooden posts. The porches cover wood-plank sidewalks with character that I can feel through my sandals. There's a hint of give in each step and a raspy squeak now and then—and these walkways lead to many saloons.

These nineteenth-century saloons are filled with relics and reminders of the colorful past: original bar tops, furniture and wood floors—walls covered with images, artifacts and tales of the renowned and the infamous who lived and died in that bygone time.

At *Bucket of Blood Saloon,* we bring our mugs of beer out to the boardwalk and lean against the hitching rail and keep an eye on the town and an ear on the storm. In *Delta Saloon,* it's a slow Tuesday night and we hang out with the bartender—he's old and Irish, with a brogue and a derby and we all raise our glasses to the women playing in the World's Cup volleyball final. In *Red Dog Saloon,* we order beer and pizza—dip buffalo wings at the bar and share stories with the bartender, who's in love with her job and the town it's in.

We eat our fill, drain our glasses and put the leftover pizza in a box—slide off the bar stools and bid the bartender, goodnight.

The town is quiet—there's only the shuffle and slap of our sandals on the sidewalk, and some indistinct chatter drifting out the open doors of saloons. No gunfights or bar brawls disturb the peace on this tranquil night—just three strange hombres passing through.

The motel lights draw us home like moths in the night. They splash their fluorescent wash across the picnic table—plenty of light for Scotty to beat Steve and me at gin rummy. The air has a tropical feel. We sit outside in T-shirts and shorts—sip a little whiskey, smoke a little weed and listen to the storm roll away.

The owners return and we chat a bit—the guy rode Harleys once upon a time. They ask if we want coffee in the morning . . . and wish us, "Goodnight."

We sit a while longer . . . and call it a day.

The heat from today has taken refuge in our room and I can't get the AC to work. The fan turns on, but the air isn't cooling and the room stays warm and muggy. I toss and turn all night.

The Bristlecone Pines

A welcome morning light appears around the edges of the curtains. I slip into my jeans and quietly leave the room. The sun has yet to clear the eastern horizon, though the air is already warm. The storm has moved on, but the sky is streaked with vibrant red and orange clouds, and their glow casts the world in a rose-color hue. It calls to mind part of an ancient rhyme: "Red sky at morning, sailors take warning," and I wonder what we might be sailing into?

The motel store is next to our room; it's unlocked but no one is in. A pot of fresh, hot coffee sits and waits, as promised. I pour a cup and take it back to our room and push open the door. The sudden onset of air and light rouse Scotty and Steve. With everyone awake and with today's threat of heat, we decide to ride before breakfast. I put the leftover pizza and three cups of motel coffee on the picnic table for our pleasure while we pack our bags and load up the motorcycles. The boys are ready first and take a final spin through town while I finish tying down my gear.

They laugh as they leave because I'm always the last to be ready to ride—at the very least, a helmet or a pair of gloves away from starting. I do my best to keep up. It's somewhat of a mystery and I smile.

As they ride back, I'm on my bike, waiting in the driveway and ready to go. I rev the engine, slip the clutch and fall in behind. We roll out of Virginia City and down the mountain, back through the nearly-ghost-towns of Gold Hill and Silver City and onto US Highway 50. We head west, toward the Sierras, cruise into Carson City and turn south at the junction onto State Route 395.

The mountains, now close at hand on our right, will journey beside us today. Riding through the valley down 395, the age of its human habitation is ever-present. We cruise along an avenue of huge and ancient cottonwood trees—we pass farms and fields of crops, green pastures with ponds and grazing animals, and through the small towns of Minden, Coleville and Walker. The road winds through a stark, rocky canyon along a narrow whitewater creek—out again and straight down the highway and into the town of Bridgeport. Without a word, signal or plan, we pull up and stop in front of the *Bridgeport Inn*. It strikes me how nonchalantly we do things—each of us accepting anyone's decision or need without question. We walk inside for breakfast.

The historic *Bridgeport Inn* is a grand hotel, with linen on the tables, good service, really good coffee and excellent biscuits and gravy. Between breakfast and a map, we decide our destination. Mammoth Hot Springs, an hour south, is mentioned. Scotty and I have each been there—I recall it as a sanctum of warmth on a cool autumn night under a bright and starry desert sky—but this week, in this heat . . . we agree, the White Mountains sound way cooler. We'll visit the Bristlecone Pines.

First, we visit the restrooms, through the hotel lobby and up a steep and narrow flight of stairs. Scotty beats me to the men's room—Scotty usually beats everyone at everything. I don't want to keep the boys waiting again and the women's room door is open. The old bathroom is clean and bright with windows and wallpaper. I feel like a distinguished guest and take special care before I leave to put the toilet seat down, give the sink a quick wipe and toss the used paper towel squarely in the trash.

To the south, the countryside opens around us—the highway climbs and falls with sweeping curves and distant views. Just north of Lee Vining at a vista point, high above Mono Lake, a tourist takes our picture with Scotty's camera while we sit sidesaddle on our motorcycles. Before leaving, we stroll a short distance down the nature trail. I've become adept at taking advantage of every stop—old bladders and long motorcycles rides.

For many miles, we ride our own ride, pulling ahead or falling behind—free-feeling cruising in the sweet spot, when the engines smooth to an effortless hum. The shiny spoke-wheels spin and roll me along—gently bobbing, without a care, on a comfortable leather seat.

We roll into Bishop and come to a stop—the heat snaps shut around us. The noonday sun blazes directly above our heads, leaving little shade anywhere and none in the street where we park. Heat from the hot asphalt radiates up and we step off our motorcycles into a great natural convection oven. I cover my new black leather seat with an old white T-shirt, and reluctantly leave the rest of the bike to bake. We quickly cross the street to *Rusty's Saloon* and Grill.

Inside, the bar is low-lit and cool—a friendly place with good beer on tap, a pool table, a dartboard and sitting alone in a corner, an old shuffleboard table. We quench our thirst with a pitcher of cold beer, shoot pool and toss darts, but it's the shuffleboard I'm drawn to—a game I've never played. The old table has a beautifully polished maple top. It awakens a childhood memory of shiny chrome-edged discs gliding smoothly down a long table—watching—too small to play. I pick up a puck and gently sail it down the glassy sea. We chill in *Rusty's* for quite a while.

Outside, the heat persists. We continue south on 395, ten miles more to Big Pine—turn east on State Route 168, a portion of one of the first transcontinental roads in America, and cruise another dozen miles to White Mountain Road. White Mountain Road is steep, narrow and twisty. I downshift twice to begin the climb and again at the start of each hairpin curve. Climbing this steep grade in low gears in the peak of the afternoon heat is too much for Scotty's bike—the coolant in the radiator begins to sputter out of the overflow and onto his leg. He pulls over kills the engine and steps off the bike. The radiator resonates with a deep rolling boil and we sit and wait while it slowly subsides.

The climb is slow. We stop often, in shade where we can, and hunker down while the motorcycles cool. We had all forgotten: the higher the elevation, the lower the boiling point. Luckily for Scotty, the coolant hitting his leg is barely scalding.

We reach a flat section of roadway with a dirt pull-out and a hiking trail. Scotty grabs his camera and we walk west along the path. From a distance, the landscape appears bleak and rocky, but it's alive with small plants—succulents and cacti with vivid yellow, orange, pink and purple flowers—a sparse, but stunning and pristine world.

Scotty has us stand for a photo and sets his camera on a rocky outcrop and sets the shutter to self-timer. He joins us and waits—the camera clicks and we return to the motorcycles.

At the 8,000-foot marker, we pass the park campground. At 10,000 feet, we reach the visitor center near the top. We park and wander into the visitor center without a clear plan of action. We need to decide about tonight. The uphill ride took longer than it should have, though we hadn't given any thought to what we might do when we got here. If we camp on the mountain, we'll need supplies—we have nothing with us, as in water or food, and none of us want to ride back down the hill, find a market, shop and make the climb again. The food choices here are meager. The ranger perceives our dilemma and she mentions a great barbeque place in Big Pine. It is tempting—we huddle a moment and decide to stay on the mountain and camp out under the stars. We'll tighten our belts, buy bottled water and bags of snacks. In kindness, the ranger offers us a can of tuna, a personal emergency ration, which I turn down. We rode up this mountain without food, water or forethought—poor planning for sure, perhaps bad luck, but not an emergency—yet.

This modern visitor's center has a small movie theatre. We buy a bag of popcorn and watch their film on The Bristlecone Pines. Some of the ancient trees are five-thousand years old and were already standing under the sun and the stars a thousand years before the pyramids. But,

I find it difficult sitting inside focusing—I would rather be out walking among the pines.

After the show we thank the ranger and leave. We walk around the outside of the building—there are bristlecone pines close at hand, just beyond the railing, scattered on the hillside. Many of them look young and have a full crop of healthy green needles, though how old they are in years or centuries, I have no idea. We decide to cruise down to the campground, unpack and then visit the bristlecone there. We wander back to the bikes, divvy up our new rations for easy hauling and roll quietly down the mountain and into the campground—loop around and find a site with gnarled old junipers and a picnic table.

We unload the bikes, saving room on the table for food, water, playing cards and whiskey... "Chuck-man, where the fuck's that weed?"

"No idea, I've checked through all my stuff twice. Scotty, you put it back in the room last night?"

"Yeah, I tossed it in on a bed."

"Hmmm... shit, what a bummer. It must've got left in Virginia City."

We go to Plan B: eat snacks, drink water and whiskey, play a hand of gin rummy and set out to explore.

Our campground occupies the floor of a small valley. An old dirt mining road runs through, east and west, along the foot of its southern hills. We walk west along the road in search of bristlecone pines—but without any luck. However, we discover that all the campsites have gnarled old junipers and picnic tables. Near the west end of the valley, we cross paths with a stranger. I stop him and ask, "Where are the all the bristlecone?"

He grins, "There aren't any bristlecone pines below 10,000 feet. Didn't you guys watch the movie? You'll have to go back up the hill and start at the Visitor's Station."

Another disappointment, but for now we continue on our way. We decide we'll visit the old pines in the morning.

The road climbs to a pass in the hills. The small valley ends here, but not the mining road. We detour out to a rocky point, a vantage point, which juts out on a western slope in the White Mountains, high above the great valley we rode through this morning. Across the valley, tall peaks of the Sierra Nevada range fill the horizon north and south, and above everything is a vast expanse of cloud-spattered sky, bright and luminous. As we linger at the scenic brink, the whole of the sky blossoms, and under a palette of brilliant yellow, we follow the road down the mountain.

Scattered along the way, we find signs of past habitation and mining activities—disintegrating mounds of rusted cans and broken bottles, scraps of building debris, flattened ground with low, crumbling stone foundations and a few pieces of abandoned machinery. The road steepens as we descend and switches back and forth—it looks as though it might snake its way all the way to the bottom of the mountain. We turn around and head back up the hill.

As we climb toward the top, I spot a mound of earth and rock that I didn't notice on the hike down. It blends in well with this lunar-like landscape of fieldstone and rocky outcrops. From the road, it has an almost natural appearance. However, in days long gone, while training as a land surveyor, I was taught to look for the "hand of man" in the environment. I walk around the little knoll and give the boys a shout. It has an opening, an entrance into a small deserted dwelling with an earthen floor a couple of feet below the ground we're standing on. We jump down into the partially subterranean shelter. Inside, the roof is domed like an igloo and is framed like the doorway with small, hand-hewn tree trunks, limbs and rocks. Along the back wall there's a raised sleeping platform also built of sticks and branches. This small earth dwelling is certainly old and might have been built by a miner, but it could be even older.

Yosemite

A car rolls past our campsite—dirt crunches beneath its tires. My eyes open to blue sky, intertwined with dark green branches. The air smells clean with a gin-like scent from the fresh-washed juniper berries growing on these resinous trees. A bubble of brightness slowly grows above the horizon to the east.

I'm wedged in tight between Steve and a tree trunk. He's buried in his bag, which is scrunched against mine and I can't get up without waking him. The two of us getting up wake Scotty a few yards away. We're all hungry and eager for breakfast. We decide to postpone our visit to the five-thousand-year-old pines. I doubt they'll miss us, but I'll miss the chance to visit with them.

The downhill ride is easy. White Mountain Road is our friend today as we coast, roll and motor our way back to Bishop. In a crowded local diner, we order biscuits and gravy, hash browns and eggs, orange juice, toast and coffee. As hungry as we are, the food is disappointing, but there's plenty of it and it's rich enough in oil and grease to fuel our ride north on 395 as we retrace yesterday's journey—fifty miles north to Lee Vining, the gateway to Yosemite.

The road out of Bishop curves west toward the Sierras. They rise before our eyes and fill the landscape. Before we reach their slopes, the road turns north again and climbs above the valley, which lies between us and the mountains—a valley rich with pasture, and bursting with morning sunshine, bright green cottonwoods, creeks and cattle. We continue north, crown the hill, and dip down into the Great Basin. Halfway to Lee Vining, the highway climbs into the Inyo National Forest, which we passed through yesterday on our journey south. The air cools quickly as we ride into the deep morning shade of the tall and thick-trunked pines. We reach another high pass and rush downhill past the only rest stop on 395 and drop once again onto the valley floor. The pines dwindle and fade away—we enter a sparse and open land, spotted with low button-like shrubs, and it's now that nature calls and with great necessity.

Humans are peculiar in this regard. Were I a coyote, a rattlesnake or a desert tortoise... but I'm not. I'm as peculiar as anyone. Regardless, Steve and Scotty are ahead in the distance and I don't want to be unknowingly left behind. I'll pull ahead of them before stopping somewhere, and walk into the desert until I'm just another spot on the horizon.

I twist the throttle open and pass Steve with a wave. The burst of acceleration tugs my body backward. I hold on tight and keep the throttle full-open. Every second counts—one-thousand-one, one-thousand-two, one-thousand three and I'm flying down the highway at the ninety miles per hour that the boys had once threatened me with and closing in fast behind Scotty. A handful of bike lengths to go and his brake light flashes red and glows bright, and he slows and stops on a short, wide section of shoulder. I squeeze and push on both brakes hard, and stiffen my arms as the bike decelerates and grinds to a halt beside him. I exhale—breath in and ask, "Scotty, what's happening?"

"My temperature light just came on." He raises his visor, tilts his head and asks with a puzzled smile, "Where'd you come from?"

Even as he speaks, something out on the bleak landscape catches my eye. I kick the side stand to the ground, step off the bike and grab a handful of tissue from my backpack. Beyond Scotty and the barbed wire highway fence, stands my salvation. Not far out in the chaparral, is a low sprawling tree in a patch of tall desert weeds.

In Lee Vining, Route 120 begins its climb into Yosemite. This junction sports a gas station, restaurant, gift shop and deli—a pit stop and hub—teeming with travelers. We gas-up and buy drinks, sit outside on top of a picnic table and warm ourselves like vultures in the morning sun. Scotty and Steve text Julie, their boss, who will call Amy, Steve's girlfriend, who will check an email and text back Jeff's address, which we hope will be our lodging tonight in El Portal.

Texting is out of my reckoning. I sit and chat with a couple of bikers and watch the day unfold. Scotty and Steve brainstorm and press buttons until they're rewarded with an address and an invitation. We finish our drinks, return to the bikes and head up the hill. The road slips in and out of mountain shadows as we wind around the steep, pine-covered slopes, which are topped with bare and jagged granite crowns.

The climb to Tioga Pass is slow today. It's peak summer travel season, just two days before the Fourth of July. Traffic barely moves as we near the top. Steve and Scotty begin weaving around cars and quickly disappear. They like to keep moving so their bikes don't overheat, but mostly, they just like to keep moving. I'm content for the moment and queue up in the long line of cars, trucks and campers—I'll save the extra effort for a must-do situation. I'm optimistically confident that the boys will be waiting somewhere near the entrance station. If not, I'll pull over: dig my flip-phone from my backpack, turn it on and find a comfortable spot to sit.

The roadway at the summit levels off and is split into several lanes with rows of traffic cones. The entrance feed-in is a quagmire. It's choked with idling vehicles. Rangers walk through, stopping at each one, collecting fees and issuing passes. Now I recall that Steve and Scotty have the paperwork that gets us in free, but it's too late—I look up and greet a Park Ranger, "Hi, I work in the Golden Gate National Recreation Area, I'm here to see a friend who works in the park."

He points to the lone empty lane on my left, which exits the park and is also separated by a long row of orange traffic cones. He points to the lane and waves towards the entrance station, "Go on through."

Life's good.

Not far beyond the station, I spot Steve and Scotty waving from a vista point. We join up once again—stand together and gaze upon a wild corner of the world where forested granite mountains tumble and fall away into a far desert valley. We decide to do some hiking, but not here—Steve has never been to Tuolumne Meadows.

We continue down Tioga Road to a signpost for the meadow—park, and hike in through a campground on a trail along a river. Beyond the pine-woods campground, we enter a dense deciduous forest—a single green canopy with countless grey trunks and the few rays of sunlight that find the forest floor. We amble along chatting and jumping mud puddles that block the path, until the woods come to a sudden end. Out from under the eaves, we step into an alpine meadow—blinking in the new-found sunshine and fresh air. The valley's floor is green, speckled with yellow flowers and peppered with stands of tall, dark pines. Down from the round-topped granite peaks at the far end, the Tuolumne River meanders towards us, rolling in its wide grey channel of huge and polished granite slabs. Spanning the river is a low wooden bridge made of heavy timbers—not exactly high ground, but a good spot to stand and survey the valley.

Steve rests a hand on my shoulder, "Chuck-man, is this it?"

"Yep, this is it."

"Cool."

We sit on a great bench-like guard rail and rest our feet comfortably on the bridge's deck as Scotty photographs the meadow.

On the hike out, clouds roll in overhead and scatter sprinkles. On the road, on our motorcycles, we ride in and out of showers. Beneath the boughs of roadside pines, we fish rain jackets and leftover snacks from our saddle bags and sit on a rocky ground garnished with pleasant-smelling pine litter.

After lunch, we work our way west in our wet-weather gear, in mostly steady rain—pass Tenaya lake and stop at a vista point. We park the bikes and walk to the edge and look out. This overlook for the distant Yosemite Valley has few sightseers on this grey and drizzly day, and little to see, except, the tops of dark and swirling clouds. Above those clouds, more clouds rush past at eye level, and it's there that I catch a glimpse of Half Dome or maybe it's El Capitan—one of the two great granite monoliths.

All day, Steve has been talking about having a beer at the *Ahwahnee Hotel,* which sits submerged beneath the storm at the far end of the Yosemite Valley. He brings it up again now, "Well, what d'you boys wanna do?"

I glance again into the darkness. It's a no-brainer. "Let's go tomorrow."

He looks down on the cloud tops and considers this a moment . . . "Buck up, boys. Let's go get a beer."

Scotty smiles—he knows Steve better than I do. We hop on our motorcycles, plunge into the storm and roll down the mountain.

On the valley floor, the rain is solid. This gloomy summer afternoon is as dim as a winter's evening. Traffic is heavy and moving erratically. Headlights burn bright, sparking glare across the dark, wet roads. My goggles fog—I stuff them in a pocket and the rain stings my eyes. I'm squinting hard and trying to keep up with Scotty as he weaves through traffic, but I can't keep up *and* watch for merging cars. I close the gap, ignore the cars and follow Scotty closely. In a tight formation, the three of us snake through the ever-shifting steel jungle. Seconds stretch into long minutes and finally Scotty slows to a stop. I lift my head, open my eyes wide and look around—relieved to see the three of us safely gathered in the parking lot of the *Ahwahnee.*

We sit a moment in the rain and admire the old *Ahwahnee Hotel,* a National Historic Landmark, nestled at the base of towering walls of granite—dark and looming now, as they disappear into the rain and clouds.

The parking lot is full, not even a spot for a motorcycle, but we find space in the duff beneath a clump of dripping sequoia, and place sticks and small rocks under the side stands to keep the bikes from sinking into the spongy surface and toppling. We walk across the lot and enter the busy hotel.

Following Steve through the lodge is somewhat of a re-run of our ride getting here. We weave through the crowded lobby, into the dining room and rush past the hostess whose greeting fades in the noise behind us—side-step waiters and guests around tables and squeeze up to the bar where there's Guinness on tap. We carry full mugs of beer back through the dining room, into the lobby, and pick our way through the packed-out museum-like hallways until we serendipitously happen on a lounge with an empty couch and a piano man, playing and singing.

We slip in out of the turbulence and onto the couch—sit back—relax—sip Guinness and clap—a welcome sojourn, this tranquil harbor, out from the stormy sea. Even on this rainy day, the great timber lodge stays warm and dry, and I watch my wet clothes steam.

The piano man takes a well-deserved break. We drain our mugs, set them on a table and leave—another place to return to on a quiet, off-season day.

Outside, the weather is almost pleasant. The storm's eye is open, and even a few uncertain patches of orange sunlight shimmer on the wet pavement, but they offer us little warmth, or hope for a dry ride much beyond the parking lot. The recently captured rainwater continues to drip down through the canopies of the big trees and onto the motorcycles. We roll them into the wavering sunlight and Scotty's bike refuses to start.

We dry the spark plugs and the wires to no avail and the storm's eye begins to close. The sky darkens and the rain returns. Scotty works diligently on his bike as Steve and I pow-wow. Steve's headlight still doesn't work and my night vision is terrible—we decide to leave now for El Portal and use what's left of the daylight, find a friend with a car and come back for Scotty and his gear. As if in protest, Scotty's Goldwing stutters and roars—the engine revs deep and strong—an unexpected and wonderful sound. Unwilling to let the engine die, Scotty shouts above the din, "I'll see you in El Portal." He snaps his helmet's visor down and rides away—before we can follow, he's gone. Steve and I scramble, grab our gear, start the bikes and swing into the saddles. He knows the way—I follow. I switch on my riding lights. They shine out into the dimness and will hopefully light both our ways in this decisive race with nightfall.

The road out of the valley is longer than my memory recalls—the rain falls harder and the evening darkens. We reach the west exit and Steve blows through the station. I slow to a roll to acknowledge the ranger in the kiosk. She looks up and I wave, she smiles kindly and looks down. I open the throttle and catch Steve.

We funnel into the narrow river gorge—the storm intensifies to a downpour—I can hardly see the road. The rain hammers and weighs me down. My mind drifts—I wonder how much farther and—POP! — I'm out of the storm and for a moment—weightless.

The roadway is dry—everything is dry. The air is warm and the strip of sky above the steep canyon walls is clear and deep blue—I see the road and the river flowing as I roll along in a dreamlike kind of bliss. We reach the town of El Portal and my clothes are dry.

El Portal is a small community just west of Yosemite on California Route 140. The streets are terraced on a steep south-facing slope above the Merced River. They're narrow, without sidewalks and connected by switchbacks. Most of the houses are unique and some have names.

We spot Scotty's bike in a dirt and gravel parking strip along the outside edge of a road. As we park, Jeff and Scotty walk around the bend. It's a much-welcomed meeting of handshakes and hugs and all the more joyous for the rough ride in.

Steve, Scotty and I unload our clothing and sleeping bags and follow Jeff back up the hill to his house. He works in Yosemite and has housing here in El Portal—a studio, built in what was once a detached garage. The main entrance is through an open carport with a roof and a concrete slab. The slab is covered with a well-worn Persian carpet, a hutch and some seating—a great front porch for just about any occasion. His house has an all-purpose room for living and sleeping, a bathroom and a small kitchen.

Jeff offers to host a dinner party with a few coworkers and mutual friends. Steve, Scotty and I walk down the hill to the El Portal Market and buy beer, salsa and chips, additional party snacks and dips and a bottle of whiskey for Jeff.

Back from the market, we sit with Jeff outside in the carport, toast our get-together with the last of Scotty's Irish whiskey and wait as friends begin to arrive—John and Mattie, Steve from Yosemite and Becky and Fiona from next door. We hang out on Jeff's front porch on this warm and sultry summer's evening—relaxing, eating, drinking, chatting, catching up and sharing stories. Our Yosemite friends are gearing up for a big Fourth of July weekend bash. They invite us to stay and hang out for the celebration. A couple more days of partying sounds fun. 'Moving on' also has a ring to it. The consensus is, we'll ride in the morning—four days on the go and it's hard to sit still.

Jeff exits the party. He disappears into his house—reappears with a large, steaming platter. The sweet, buttery aroma of sautéed prawns and garlic spills over us.

"Mmmm."

"Wow." and the likes of such, echo throughout the gathering.

He sets the platter down and the big shrimp vanish.

The talk slows and softens as the evening wears on—one by one, the good folk say good night and wander home. I sit on the carpet, rest my back against a wall and stretch my legs out flat . . . my head nods and rebounds. My eyes spring open to see Becky and Steve looking down with a smile. I smile in return, and think—*It's been a long day. It might even be tomorrow.*

Becky walks to her home next door and now all the guests are gone. Steve, Scotty, Jeff and I haul any leftover drinks and food (there's not much of either) inside. Jeff offers to cook up a breakfast in the morning. We accept tomorrow's offer and thank him for tonight—toss our sleeping bags down on the carport carpet, curl up inside them and crash.

I get up in the night and find a quiet spot along the rustic hillside hedgerow. The evening is still warm. Drifting patches of thin, high clouds randomly sprinkle their few remaining drops of rain—big, lazy drops that *plop* when they land on my head or hit the ground.

Home

The morning dawns clear and mostly quiet. Tweep-tweep... tweep-tweep. The after-the-rain air is fresh and clean. Scotty and Steve are still asleep and Jeff's house is entirely quiet. I slip out of my sleeping bag and into my pants, put on my T-shirt and sandals and walk down the hill to check on the motorbikes. The day is too hot for this early in the morning. Steam rises from the street as the sun peeks through the trees and climbs over the houses. The motorcycles are draped in shade, still wet from the rain and covered with big beads of clear water. I wipe my bike down—paint, leather and chrome. The boys' bikes are partially covered with a tarp. I remove it so the engines can breathe, and give them a wipe as well. I shuffle back up the driveway to the carport and Steve and Scotty stir in their bags.

I call out quietly, "Good morning."
Steve returns a raspy, "Chuck-man."
Scotty, a groggy, "Hey."
"You guys wanna grab some coffee at the market?" I ask.
Scotty lifts his head, "Sounds good."
They exchange their sleeping bags for shorts and sandals. The house is still quiet—we slip away and walk down the hill to a hiking trail that

Jeff pointed out yesterday—a shortcut that bypasses the last switchback and drops us off at the back of the market. The store carries much of what a small community might need in the way of groceries, alcohol, custom silkscreened baseball caps and Yosemite souvenirs. The back room has a lounge area with couches, pastries and pots of fresh coffee. We help ourselves to the coffee—sit and enjoy some small-talk and quiet time.

With empty stomachs and the coffee buzzing, we retrace our steps back up the trail to the roadway and driveway, through the carport and to the house—the front door is open wide. We step across the threshold and the smoky smell of frying bacon greets us. Jeff also greets us from his kitchen as he sips coffee and munches bacon. A platter of the crispy strips is cooling on the counter and we all hang out in the ship-like galley and polish them off with OJ and coffee. Jeff scrambles eggs and fries up tomatoes—we toast and butter bread. Everything is cooked and ready to eat and we fill our plates with the food that's left, shuffle a few steps to the living room to a couch or a chair.

Sitting on the coffee table is a photo of Jeff on a mountainside. He describes the thrills and intricacies of rock climbing, hang gliding and paragliding. We discuss surfing, windsurfing and archery, and other adventures of man and womankind. The conversation morphs to ancient and alien civilizations, and on and into stranger realms. We breakfast and talk until the food is gone—clean up and pack our bags, and thank our good host for his hospitality.

With our hands and arms loaded with gear, the four of us trudge down the hill to where our motorcycles sit and wait, glinting in the morning sunshine. They're dry and clean and they start right up. With everything stowed and tied securely, we give Jeff a final hug, hop on the bikes and roll down the hill onto Route 140. I enjoy the morning starts the most—the first ride of the day—we're fresh (usually), happy and eager to be on the road again and off on another adventure.

We reach the foothill's town of Mariposa mid to late morning and pull to a stop in front of a market. Today is already unreasonably hot. It portends to be the hottest day of this trip. Our water bottles are full but we buy three quarts of cold Gatorade for insurance—cross the street to an auto parts store and buy eight cooler-running spark plugs for the boys' *Goldwings*—additional insurance.

While gassing up at the local Chevron, we spread our road map across the motorcycles and debate whether we should take Route 49 north. The guy at the next pump blurts out, "Definitely! People come from all over the world to ride motorcycles on that road."

Not many miles out of Mariposa, we pull under a sprawling black oak in a gravelly turnout. The day is heating rapidly and we're already parched. We dig out our quarts of Gatorade, which are losing their chill and gulp down some of the bright green, lemon-lime liquid. While we're parked in the shade and before the day gets hotter, we decide to install the new spark plugs in the *Goldwings*, even though their exhaust pipes are singing . . . *tink* . . . *tink* . . . *tink* . . . as the heat leaves the hot metal. We manage to do it anyway and without any serious burns.

Route 49 proves to be true to the stranger's advice. They're James

Bond movie-miles with perfectly banked curves along newly-paved and super-smooth roadways, on the edge of steep and pristine canyons. On any other day, it could be an exhilarating ride, but today is unmercifully hot and we ride along half in a daze.

On the outskirts of Sonora, we veer onto a side road and stop at a small, town park. Without the wind of our moving motorcycles, beads of sweat drip from our red and over-heated faces. We sit in the shade on some cool, stone steps, where Steve finds a wallet with local ID. While passing around a bottle of lukewarm water, we decide, we'll walk to town, find cold drinks, and a place where we can turn in the wallet. It's a short, hot walk on the south end of town to a small strip mall with an air-conditioned supermarket. Right inside sitting on a table, is a big glass cooler filled with water and ice and slices of lemons and oranges. Next to that is a tall stack of small, waxed paper cups. We drink our fill and make several slow passes through the frozen food aisles—buy cold drinks and exit into the heat.

A couple of doors down in a small local bank, we hand over the wallet. I explain to the teller, "We found this in the park." But she doesn't feel like dealing with it.

She flips it open, looks inside, snaps it shut and tries to hand it back, complaining, "Well, I don't know her either."

I put my finger on the window and point to her countertop, "You have a telephone and we're just passing through." We turn around and leave the bank.

Steve gives my shoulder a shake, "Way to hold your ground."

I smile and point out, "No wonder the place is empty." He and

Scotty smile, too.

We walk back to the bikes, toss the empty bottles in a city recycle bin and continue riding north on Route 49—through the historic gold mining town of Angels Camp, written of in Mark Twain's short story, *"The Celebrated Jumping Frog of Calaveras County"*—through the rustic countryside, past farms and houses and into the town of San Andreas. At the north end of town, we veer west onto Highway 12 and gradually descend into the Central Valley. I feel like Dante.

A dozen miles out of San Andreas, in the small town of Valley Springs, we pull into the parking lot for the 1-4-5 *Club Steakhouse and Bar*. We walk inside. It's mid-afternoon and except for a bartender, the place looks empty. The bartender greets us and we sit at the bar and ask her what beers they have on hand. Bottles rattle as she looks through the cooler—she gives us our choices and we each pick a beer. She pours the cold beer into ice-cold mugs and we don't say much for a minute or two. With the worst of our thirst quenched, we mention lunch, and she hands us menus describing tasty-sounding sandwiches. In between sips we place an order. She takes it to the kitchen and returns to the bar.

The four of us talk small talk, sharing stories of our homes and travels. She's a local girl, born and raised in Valley Springs, and she asks us playfully, with maybe a hint of whimsy, "Will you guys take me with you?"

We smile in answer. She's a good bartender and knows how to flatter three road-weary bikers. We drink and talk and wait for our food.

The cook brings out our lunches, his name is Lee—he's also the owner and the food is as good as its description. While we sit and eat, the five of us chat. Lee was a backup musician in the 1970's for *The Drifters* and for other groups as well. He plays guitar, drums and saxophone. Steve and I are band-mates in *Blues Whale,* a funky jam band out of the Marin Headlands and Scotty plays a banjo. We all talk music for a while.

With our lunches finished to the last drop of beer, it's time to leave and finish our travels—although reality is setting in and I'm feeling reluctant to end this trip, but even less willing to postpone the inevitable—we say goodbye.

The road home is essentially west, but it follows the meanderings of old Route 12—across the Central Valley past its farms, vineyards and fruit tree orchards—through the towns of Clements, Lockeford and Lodi, under route 99 and I-5, over the Sacramento River via the Rio Vista Bridge and into downtown Rio Vista.

Rio Vista is a delta town. We park on Main Street and walk across to *Foster's Bighorn,* a landmark bar and restaurant. Inside, every wall is filled with trophies, the heads of animals from around the world. Most of them lived in Africa or North America, and most were killed in the 1930s. We sit at the end of the very long bar, order three glasses of light draft beer and look around at the once living, but still noble beasts. Scotty lifts a hand and waves it through the air and asks, "What's this all about?" His question goes unanswered and we sit in silence. I'm haunted by the guilt and shame of human recklessness for all this unnecessary loss. We raise our glasses in a final toast, drain them and leave.

It's early evening, we're near the water's edge, yet the heat of the day persists almost unabated. All day, I say to the boys, "It'll cool as we ride west."

All day they ask, "When?"

We get on our bikes to leave. Scotty points to the corner store sign, "Check it out." The sign flashes . . . 5:00 PM . . . 99°F.

"Look!" I shout, "It's only 5 o'clock and it's already under a hundred."

We take Main Street out of town and merge back onto Highway 12 and skirt along the northern edges of low, rolling hills of golden grasses. These hills are farms and they harvest the wind—hundreds of tall metal towers with spinning blades and turbines gather power from the unrelenting force that we now battle head-on. It's a rough and ragged ride to Fairfield—one of the most wearing of the journey. We roll into a gas station on the east end of town just beyond the 'Welcome to Fairfield' sign, and I wonder how it got its name, but at the moment, I'm just glad to be out of its wind. I pull up to a pump, hop off the bike and put a credit card in the reader, "I got it."

"Chuck-man, your debt is paid—we're all good."

"No, this is it, last one and we'll be square."

In truth, no one's been keeping count, but for the second time today, within this hour, I'm feeling guilty. I won't be riding back to Marin with the boys and seeing them through to the end of their ride—we'll soon be parting ways. Each of us has someone waiting somewhere. Mallory and Amy are in the Headlands, my wife Daphne and my dog Pete in Napa. It's been a fun journey—a brief binge, living a bohemian life, without judgement or care.

We pull out of the gas station and into the wind, but its force dies quickly as we approach the hills that border I-80. It's a short jog west on the Interstate to the Napa exit, and a smooth, fast ride along the new four-lane highway through Jamison Canyon. North on 29, west on 121/12 and we're almost back to the Fremont diner, where we met four and a half days ago. All too soon, we reach my turnoff—I beep and wave as Steve and Scotty pull away toward their home in the Marin Headlands. Our friendships were solid at the start of this trip—more so now that we share something unique. I catch a final glimpse of them as they fade into the west. They seem invincible—on or off a motorcycle, more capable than me.

 Alone again, I retrace the backroads where my solo journey began—into the vineyard valley and past the tree-lined pastures of grazing livestock—*do they ever not graze?* It's the same place—the green vines and the blue sky above the golden hills—though now it basks in a different light, the glow of the late-day sun. My old-school open face helmet allows in all the smells that fill the air on this warm summer's evening—the hay-like scent from the fields of yellow grasses, the minty, aromatic leaves and bark piled deep along a row of eucalyptus, the sharp, but not unpleasant tang of tar wafting from the hot roadway. The warm air whisks around me—flaps and fills my shirt—scrubs, dries and gently massages. Quietly cruising and rolling along, the journey is *definitely* half the fun.

 I arrive home and pull into the driveway, turn off the ignition and the gas to the carburetors—push the bike into the garage and rock it back onto its center stand. The odometer reads a thousand miles more than it did at the start of this trip. Somehow, a thousand-mile journey seems perfect.

 I'm tired but relaxed, nostalgically blue and in need of a shower. I take off my shoes, open a side case and pull out my sandals. I'm standing barefoot in the same spot I stood early Monday morning—the same spot, but perhaps, a bit further along.

I'll unpack the bike tomorrow and bring Pete to help—he can examine the scents on my unwashed and well-traveled clothes, the camping gear, the dusty shoes and the dirt in the grooves of the tires—an abundance of smells to explore and experience, and maybe he can vicariously enjoy a taste of the places they've traveled.

Epilogue

In the spring of 2016, Steve received his Master's degree from San Francisco State University. He took a summer job teaching marine biology on a sailing ship and set sail from Ireland. After his tour, he met up with Amy and they traveled through Europe stopping in The Czech Republic to visit our friends Reece and Lucie, Reece being a former band-mate of Blues Whale. In the fall, Steve signed on to a fishing boat and worked through the winter off the coast of Alaska. In the spring of 2017, he returned to the Marin Headlands where he now works and lives.

In August of 2017, Mallory and Scotty were married in the small California coastal community of Stinson Beach. The ceremony and reception were held outside on a terraced hillside above the sea. There was dining and dancing under the stars with many, friends to celebrate— the band jammed and the night rocked.

Later that night, with the wedding reception over, in the stillness and quiet of the after-midnight hours, a streak of light whistles into the sky, high above the rolling surf—bursts and blossoms silver-white—booms, echoes and rains down sparkling—a finale fitting this night of celebration on a midsummer's night in the fiftieth year of the *'Summer of Love.'*

www.ingramcontent.com/pod-product-compliance
Lightning Source LLC
Chambersburg PA
CBHW061145010526
44118CB00026B/2872